COOL CAREERS
WITHOUT COLLEGE
FOR PEOPLE WHO LOVE TO
ENTERTAIN

COOL CAREERS
WITHOUT COLLEGE
FOR PEOPLE WHO LOVE TO
ENTERTAIN

AMIE JANE LEAVITT

ROSEN
PUBLISHING®

New York

To my nieces and nephews, the most entertaining troupe I know.

Published in 2017 by The Rosen Publishing Group, Inc.
29 East 21st Street, New York, NY 10010

Library of Congress Cataloging-in-Publication Data

Names: Leavitt, Amie Jane, author.
Title: Cool careers without college for people who love to entertain / Amie Jane Leavitt.
Description: New York : Rosen Publishing, 2017. | Series: Cool careers without college | Includes bibliographical references and index.
Identifiers: LCCN 2016018106 | ISBN 9781508172741 (library bound)
Subjects: LCSH: Acting—Vocational guidance—Juvenile literature. | Entertainers—Vocational guidance—Juvenile literature.
Classification: LCC PN2055 .L43 2017 | DDC 792.02/8023—dc23
LC record available at https://lccn.loc.gov/2016018106

Manufactured in Malaysia

CONTENTS

INTRODUCTION

So, you want to find a career and not just a job, but you don't have the time, interest, or money to attend a four-year university? That's OK, because there are many careers out there that don't require a bachelor's degree, especially in the entertainment industry.

If you think the entertainment industry just involves what you see on television or in the movies, then you're only thinking inside the box. The careers in this industry are widespread, including everything from what you see on the silver screen, small screen, and stage to what you don't get to view that goes on behind the scenes. Think about the clothing people wear on television: the actors didn't just show up wearing that apparel. It was all carefully chosen by someone behind the scenes. The sets

Some people are just born to entertain, like this female jazz singer performing in a night club. Others want to be a part of creating the magic that audiences flock to see. Do you dream of a job in the entertainment industry, too?

might look like real houses in movies and television, but that's just an allusion. They're all fake places, built specifically for filming purposes. A specialist behind the scenes had to build those, too. Think about the special effects that you see and hear while watching a commercial, movie, or television show. Those effects don't just magically happen. They're all created by someone who has a specific behind-the-scenes job in the entertainment industry. While it's certainly true that many people in the entertainment industry are creative types, they're also proficient technicians, builders, and organizers, too.

This resource will explore ten careers in the entertainment industry. The purpose of the book is to give you a little background information on each career and some ideas for different ways to pursue those careers so you can explore new ideas on your own. The main goal here is to help you become a thinker and an entrepreneur. Really, both of those skills are crucial when it comes to finding jobs in the entertainment industry. Many people want to be in show business, and because of that, the market is highly saturated. For every job opening, there are dozens and dozens of people applying. In order to make it in the entertainment industry, you must be an inventive thinker. You must think of ways that you can find jobs that will put you steps ahead of other people.

People are often leery of choosing careers in the entertainment industry because they don't want to be a "starving artist." However, these careers can actually be just as lucrative as any other. You can make good money at any of the jobs listed in this book. Just like anything else, these jobs are what you make of them. There is a better chance for success if you dive in with all the initiative, determination, and savvy that you can muster!

CHAPTER 1

WORKING AS A MUSICIAN OR SINGER

You're listening to your favorite band. As you do, you dream of what it would be like to be a famous musician with wealth, fans, and celebrity status. Many people have dreams of stardom like this, but the reality is that few people actually achieve that dream. Bands pop up around the world every day. A few make it all the way to the top, but many do not. With that reality in mind, is it impossible to think you could make a living as a musician or singer? Not necessarily—you just have to be a little more creative in your approach, that's all. If you think that you will just record a song and magically have it land on the radio

Musicians are often hired to perform at weddings and other special events. You must look outside the box to find gigs in this industry. Many preformers and technicians pursue multiple forms of work in order to do what they love and earn a good living.

Not all entertainment jobs involve entertaining people! Some allow you to use your musical skills to teach others.

where you'll become the next big hit, then you're most likely going to be disappointed. But if you're willing to look outside the box with this career, then it actually is possible to make a go of it. You may not end up being hugely famous, but it is possible to make a living and support yourself as a musician or singer.

There are many types of jobs that musicians and singers can pursue in the entertainment industry. One option is to work as a singer or musician for weddings, parties, or special events. Another option for jobs in this industry is to work in a music studio or music store. Musicians and singers also work in theaters, orchestras, and symphonies. Jobs like these often require advanced training and possibly even college, but they're still worth looking into. If you have interests in traveling the world, you should consider becoming a musician or singer on a cruise ship. This is an often overlooked opportunity to use your musical talents. Of course, there are pros and cons to working on a cruise ship.

The hours will be long, you will likely have to perform the same type of music over and over again, and you will spend months at sea. However, you will also get to see some amazing places on the planet all while doing what you love. Another type of job that musicians and singers can find is in a religious setting. Praise bands are increasing in popularity, and all of those musicians are paid for their work during worship services. In many worship congregations, musicians such as organists, choir members, and quartets are also paid for their performances.

Singers and musicians might:

- Perform music for an audience or for a recording with voice or a musical instrument.
- Travel, as jobs are not always found in your geographic area.
- Audition for bands, events, and performance venues.

Want to make a few extra coins while performing your music? Open your guitar case, set up shop in a subway station, and start to play and sing! You'll be able to get a good sense of how others react to your skills.

INTERVIEW WITH MUSICIAN APRIL MESERVY

April Meservy began singing semiprofessionally when she was seventeen and started taking on studio vocal work. She began writing a year or so later, with some opportunities to write music for a couple of small projects. It was around this time she began playing around her area with her band, starting with covers and eventually adding original music. Now, her work is a mix of projects: studio vocal work, touring, and live shows, which range from festivals and city events to weddings and corporate events with her jazz quartet. She also relies on CD/album sales, royalties, and producing other artists' albums, singles, and other vocal production.

Meservy says some of her favorite jobs have involved travel. "I loved being hired to sing in China — it was an incredible opportunity and I met many wonderful people. I was once flown to Long Beach, California, with a killer band to record a music video in an airplane hangar. I've loved touring." But other work expands her range and technical ability, like studio vocal work in different styles and languages. What makes the career so challenging is the constant hustle. She explains, "Singer-songwriters these days have to be very creative—and we usually have income from several different sources. It takes a lot of hard work, but it makes life more exciting."

- Rehearse music often, either alone or with your performing group, and sometimes daily.
- Develop marketing skills to promote your music.

Musicians and singers can also use their talents to teach others. Teachers in schools need to have college degrees, of course. However, private teachers do not. You could start your own music studio where you provide instruction on instruments (violin, cello, harp, piano, trumpet) or in vocal training. Music teachers can help students train for work on the stage or for auditions. People who love music can also either work as an employee in a music store or be an entre-preneur and open their own music store.

PREPARING YOURSELF

While a college education is not necessary to become a singer or musician, musical training of some kind definitely is. If you have a great voice, you might be able to record your own YouTube video without any kind of tutelage. However, most people have to take at least some lessons in order to get a good foundation. Private lessons are one idea, or you can take music classes in school. Take advantage of these opportunities, and learn as much as you can from your teachers. Offer to work as a teacher's assistant if you want some extra experience. You can also find out if your town has community musical programs. Some communities have bands and choral groups that allow people to join for free. These types of opportunities will give you experience playing music in a group and in front of an audience.

FUTURE PROSPECTS

The US Bureau of Labor Statistics indicates that the job market for musicians and singers is expected to grow only 3 percent between 2014 and 2024. This is lower than average for other occupations. So, with these kinds of job prospects on the horizon, if you want to become a musician or singer, you will definitely need to be creative in your approach. Some other ideas that this report gives for future job needs include playing instruments for musical scores for commercials, films, and television; singing backup for recordings of other artists in the studio or while they're on tour; serving as a session musician (playing backup instruments in a studio setting); and singing backup for commercials, films, and television.

FOR MORE INFORMATION

BOOKS

Russell, Matthew J. *Careers in Music: How to Get a Job as a Cruise Ship Musician*. Amazon Digital Services, 2013.
The author tells how to find a job as a musician on a cruise ship, based on his own experiences. He worked as a pianist on cruise ships for more than six years, and during that time he visited seven continents.

Tortorella, Neil. *Starting Your Career as a Musician*. New York, NY: Allworth Press, 2013.
Neil Tortorella has been a guitarist since he was thirteen. In this book, he helps aspiring artists find their own path, with advice on what to watch out for and ways to encounter more success in the music industry.

Weisman, Loren. *Music Business for Dummies*. Hoboken, NJ: John Wiley & Sons, 2015.
This particular "Dummies" title explains life as working as a musician. It covers copyrights, publishing, royalties, recording, performing, rehearsing, and entering the online music world, among other topics.

ORGANIZATIONS

American Federation of Musicians of the United States
and Canada (AFM)
14 Penn Plaza, 12th Floor
PO Box 2673
New York, NY 10117-0262
(800) 833-8065 Ext. 1311
Website: http://www.afm.org
Founded in 1896, AFM is the largest organization in
the world dedicated to the interests of musicians. They
help negotiate contracts, offer health and insurance
programs, and provide opportunities for collaboration.

Future of Music Coalition (FMC)
2217 14th Street NW, 2nd Floor
Washington, DC 20009
(202) 822-2051
Website: http://futureofmusic.org
FMC was founded in 2000 and works with musicians,
composers, and other industry professionals. Their
goal is to support "a musical ecosystem where artists
flourish and are compensated fairly and transparently
for their work."

APPS

Teunuto
This app offers a selection of exercises to improve your
understanding of music and music theory.

WEBSITES

Due to the changing nature of internet links, Rosen
Publishing has developed an online list of websites
related to the subject of this book. This site is updated
regularly. Please use this link to access the list:

http://www.rosenlinks.com/CCWC/enter

CHAPTER 2

WORKING AS AN ACTOR

People often think of acting as what they see on television and in movies. This is an important part of the industry, but there are many other opportunities available for people who have the acting bug. Finding a job as an actor requires resourcefulness and creativity. One option for jobs in the acting world is on the stage. Actors can perform in Broadway and Broadway-style theaters, community theaters, children's theaters, amusement parks, cruise ships, Las Vegas–style shows, and in comedy routines. Another option is on the screen, but not necessarily in television shows. Commercials need actors. Production studios need extras, who are "filler" background actors with nonspeaking parts. Some of these jobs are paid a decent fee, some are paid just a little,

Actors often have to learn other skills besides just memorizing lines. Often the job is extremely physical, with routines, staging, and long practice hours. These teens are practicing some dance moves they'll do in their next show.

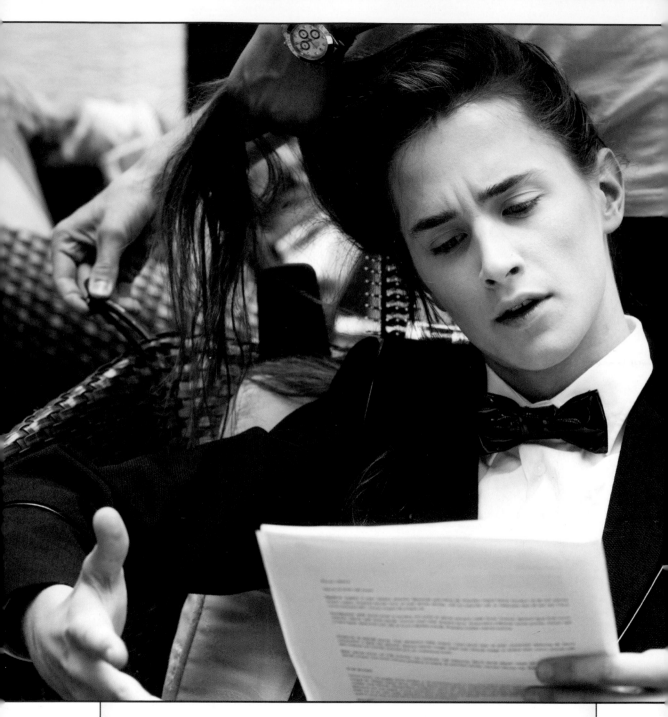

It takes a great deal of dedication and concentration to memorize lines for a show. This skill can be honed the more you practice it.

and some are not paid at all. At the beginning of your career, you may need to take jobs that pay very little or not at all in order to build your résumé and portfolio. As you are starting out, you may need to:

- Audition for parts by reading scripts in front of producers, directors, or agents.
- Research the part as much as possible so the performance is believable.
- Memorize, memorize, memorize.
- Rehearse alone and with the rest of the cast.
- Perform the show (theater, commercial, television, movie).
- Develop marketing skills to promote youself in the business and get your name known.
- Take lessons when necessary to improve craft, including skills like dancing, singing, or comedy.
- Travel to on-location jobs away from home.

It's difficult to be shy and be an actor. You'll have to be up in front of others performing your lines during the real show and during rehearsal.

Actors have a variety of responsibilities in their jobs. They must frequently audition for parts and must be able to present themselves in a confident manner. Actors must also be versatile since every part they try out for will be different from the last. They must have the ability to memorize scripts as well as make time to meet with agents, research characters, rehearse, work with voice coaches (when their characters speak different dialects or accents), and then finally perform their roles. Actors don't just work a standard nine-to-five schedule, either. Sometimes they work all day long and late into the evening, depending upon the project. Traveling to various locations for work can be part of the job, as is being gone from home for months at a time.

The online world also presents many opportunities for actors. YouTube is a fantastic option for actors to create videos which can be viewed and shared through social media. Vine, a platform that features six-second videos, is also hugely popular. For example, as of 2016, Brittany Furlan was the third- most-popular Vine user with more than ten million followers. She had moved to Los Angeles from Philadelphia to become an actor, but it wasn't working out. She had difficulty finding jobs, as many actors discover when they arrive in

INTERVIEW WITH ACTOR CHARAN PRABHAKAR

Charan Prabhakar got into the acting business in 2004 when he was living in Utah. He enrolled in an acting class and started networking with filmmakers. Networking has driven his career: "I went to film festivals, met other filmmakers, volunteered to work on people's projects for free, etc. Then I got into an acting class, became friends with other actors, started working with them. I eventually got an agent which helped me audition for more jobs." He worked in film, doing movies and commercials, and after moving to Los Angeles five years later began picking up TV work.

To Prabhakar, the most difficult thing about acting is dealing with the audition process and the inevitable rejection. His advice to young actors outside of networking is to create your own content and opportunities for work, which gives beginners a portfolio to showcase their talents. "I can't tell you how many jobs I booked because someone somewhere saw something I did online and wanted me to do work for them," he says. "It's pretty powerful stuff."

Hollywood. So, in Furlan's spare time, she started making these short Vine videos: they became a hit! In fact, she became so popular that in March 2015 she was named by *Time* magazine as one of the thirty most influential people on the internet. And this was all because of her comedic six-second videos on Vine and her marketing techniques on other social media platforms.

PREPARING YOURSELF

Actors do not have to go to college. However, they often do take advantage of other types of training such as workshops, private mentoring by drama coaches, acting lessons, and so forth. Depending upon the roles, actors may also need to have training in dance or singing, too, especially if they are performing in Broadway-style theater. Some of this training can be obtained while teens are still in high school. Drama is a class that is offered at most high schools, and many high schools also have both small and large stage productions. Often high schools also offer film, dance, and music classes, too. High school students should take advantage of all of these opportunities. Many areas also have community theaters with roles for characters of all ages. Even little children can take part in these productions as background characters or lead roles. With all of these opportunities, you may not get a starring role, but even a minor or "cast" role will give you experience on the stage and help you improve your acting abilities.

Budding actors should also work on developing some of their "nonacting" qualities, too, as they prepare for an acting career. Research skills are needed to find out more about characters, settings, and time periods. These skills are also crucial when it comes to finding jobs. Creativity is also an obvious requirement. Actors need memorization skills, reading skills, and speaking skills. In addition, they need to know how to transform themselves into a completely different person or character. Actors must also use their creativity when it comes to obtaining work, too.

FUTURE PROSPECTS

The US Bureau of Labor Statistics projects that acting jobs will increase 10 percent between 2014 and 2024. This is faster than average for all occupations (which are expected to increase an average of only 7 percent). This increase is partly because of the different medias that production companies are planning on using, such as on-demand videos and online television.

Even though there is an expected increase in the number of jobs, it's important to note that there is also intense competition in the acting industry.

FOR MORE INFORMATION

BOOKS

Jackson, Kym. *The Hollywood Survival Guide for Actors: Your Handbook to Becoming a Working Actor in LA.* Chicago, IL: RR Donnelley, 2013.

Jackson is an actress who shares recommendations for how to make it in Hollywood. Jackson shares her own advice and the advice of other professionals in the industry in this 352-page tome.

Kerr, Judy. *Acting is Everything: An Actor's Guidebook for a Successful Career in Los Angeles.* Studio City, CA: September Publishing, 2006.

The author of this book is an accomplished actress as well as an acting and dialogue coach. She uses her extensive career experience to teach readers how to prepare for success and live their dream.

O'Neil, Brian. *Acting as a Business, Fifth Edition: Strategies for Success.* New York, NY: Vintage, 2014.

Written by a former talent agent and personal manager who has represented actors in theater, television, commercials, and radio, the book details guidelines that actors can use to find success in the industry.

Port, Michael. *Steal the Show: From Speeches to Job Interviews to Deal-Closing Pitches, How to Guarantee a Standing Ovation for All the Performances in Your Life.* New York, NY: Houghton Mifflin, 2015.
This book goes beyond basic acting advice to help readers find ways to improve performances in all parts of their lives. The emphasis is on speeches, job interviews, and deal-closing pitches.

ORGANIZATIONS

Actors Equity Association, National Headquarters (AEA)
165 West 46th Street
New York, NY 10036
(212) 869-8530
Website: http://www.actorsequity.org
Founded in 1913, AEA is a labor union that represents actors and stage managers. It helps negotiate wages, improve working conditions, and provides health benefits and pension plans to members.

Sundance Institute
1825 Three Kings Drive
Park City, UT 84060
(435) 658-3456
Website: http://www.sundance.org
The Sundance Institute promotes and encourages the production of independent films, especially through the Sundance Film Festival. It was founded by Robert Redford at his Sundance Ski Resort in Provo, Utah.

WEBSITES

Due to the changing nature of internet links, Rosen Publishing has developed an online list of websites related to the subject of this book. This site is updated regularly. Please use this link to access the list:

http://www.rosenlinks.com/CCWC/enter

Rodeo clowns are tasked with very important responsibilities: they entertain as a clown and protect as a bullfighter. Their performances often include using slapstick comedy routines, acrobatics, tricks with animals, goofy dances, and vaudeville-style sketches. Rodeo clown Keith Isley uses a variety of animal sidekicks in his performances, including a miniature horse, a full-size horse, and a dog. His dog will "play dead" then hop back up and run through a maze of barrels. His horses will behave as if they're dogs by rolling over, playing fetch, and picking up ropes and hats. His hilarious routines helped him win the title of PRCA Clown of the Year from 2006 to 2011.

Rodeo clowns generally paint their faces in typical clown style and dress up in silly clothes, usually with a western flair. There's no set wardrobe, but many will wear such things as cowboy hats, brightly colored fringed western-style shirts, overalls, oversized jeans

Rodeo clowns serve as entertainers and as bull fighters, or diversions, for bull riders. While they are sometimes considered old fashioned, they still thrive in many parts of the United States.

with suspenders, tall colorful socks, and bandanas. As a rodeo clown, you must:

- Make people laugh with slapstick type routines.
- Keep the bull riders safe by distracting the bull.
- Stay physically fit and quick on your feet in order to perform dangerous stunts in the ring.
- Develop marketing abilities to get your name known in the business through a website, interviews, and networking.
- Learn how to do clown hair and makeup and wear rodeo clown-style costumes.
- Travel to rodeos located throughout the country during the season.

Besides making people laugh, another important responsibility of a rodeo clown is to act as a diversion for bull-riding cowboys. Once a cowboy is thrown from a bull, it's the rodeo clown's job to divert the bull's attention so that the cowboy can get out of the ring safely. This is done

Rodeo clowns must exude courage—they frequently find themselves eye to eye and toe to toe with charging bulls. It can be a dangerous profession, but those who do it find it very rewarding.

in all kinds of ways, like taunting the bull and getting the animal to charge toward the clown. When that happens, the rodeo clown will try to leap over the fence, hide behind an obstacle, or jump inside a barrel. They'll even get up close to the bull and run alongside the animal in its blind spot. The bull won't be able to see the clown in its peripheral vision, so the clown stays safe even at this close proximity.

The third responsibility of rodeo clown work is for the rodeo clown to stay safe himself. To do this, he uses his lifetime of experience working with bulls and spends time with the bull's owner to find out the temperament of the particular animal he'll be working with. He can also make sure to take care of his own body by eating right and staying in shape. Both are necessary for the intense stunt work that he'll do out in the ring.

A steady hand along with a steady head is needed for a rodeo clown career. Putting on your own makeup is generally part of the job.

PREPARING YOURSELF

Many rodeo clowns start young and learn the rodeo clown business by apprenticing with other rodeo clowns. This is a common way to learn the ins and outs of the job. Prospective rodeo clowns can learn the business by apprenticing at small local rodeos and at youth rodeo events. Another way to learn the trade is to attend rodeo schools which offer in-the-ring courses on bullfighting. One school is the Sankey Rodeo School. It teaches rodeo athletes how to ride bulls (for the cowboys) and bullfight (for the clowns). The courses are taught to youths and adults in locations all over the country from rural to urban areas. The company even teaches a three-day course at Madison Square Garden in New York City. Another way that people learn the trade is by continuing to study after they've become a rodeo clown. In a 2009 *Forbes* article, "Inside the Life of a Rodeo Clown," rodeo clown Dusty Tuckness explains, "In my off time, I review film of some of my own work and some from the great old names to see how they pulled things off." To develop their routines, rodeo clowns also keep up on current events in the news and on social media. Their jokes have to come from somewhere, and most rodeo clowns find that often real life is funnier than anything they could make up themselves.

IT'S A DANGEROUS JOB BUT . . .

Bullfighting of any kind is a dangerous job, so rodeo clown work definitely has its tense moments. One dangerous moment happened for Timber Tuckness. In a ring in North Dakota, he hopped in a barrel for protection from a charging bull. The bull's leg got stuck inside the barrel and it kicked ferociously to get free. However, the kicking didn't just hit the side of the barrel. Most of the impact was on Tuckness's head. He ended up with a three-month recovery period because of a broken jaw and broken neck.

Even though there are serious risks involved with this line of work, it's a dream job for many who pursue it. Tuckness, for one, is a third-generation rodeo clown. "My grandparents were in the rodeo," he told *Forbes* magazine in 2009. "My mother was a trick-rider. I was born to do this." Even his son Dusty, who entered the ring at age eleven, is now working as a rodeo clown. Many rodeo clowns are drawn by the action, the love of being in front of a crowd, and the chance to travel the country doing a different rodeo every night. Rodeo clown Justin Rumford told the *Las Vegas Sun* in 2012, "I like traveling; I like working with crowds. I like rodeo people. They're good folks. Every weekend, it's a new place. It just doesn't get old."

FUTURE PROSPECTS

Most rodeo clowns are self-employed. They build their business with savvy marketing techniques, by networking with rodeo organizers, and by developing a solid reputation. Rodeo clowns generally work on a per-show basis and set their own fees. The more experienced and well-known you are, of course, the more money you can charge. Many rodeo clowns will work hundreds of rodeos throughout rodeo season (which lasts from spring through fall).

The US Department of Labor does not collect employment data on rodeo clowns, so it's difficult to know expected job growth in this industry. Rodeos seem to be staples of entertainment, so there will certainly still be a need for rodeo clowns in the near future. One difficulty for rodeo clowns is securing health insurance. Insurance companies generally do not like insuring people in dangerous occupations—they don't want to have to pay all of those medical bills. However, according to the Affordable Care Act, everyone must be insured or pay a fine. So, rodeo clowns often just have to pay a fine if they can't find a company willing to take them on, and then pay for all of their hospital expenses on their own. This is something to keep in mind when considering a career as a rodeo clown.

FOR MORE INFORMATION

BOOKS

Dix, Bog and Lynette Dix. *"ACTION!" John 'Bud' Cardos: The True Story of a Renaissance Cowboy, Rodeo Clown, Actor, Stuntman, and Director in Hollywood.* Benson, AZ: L & B Publishing, 2016.
This book tells the story of John "Bud" Cardos, who was a famous rodeo clown and renaissance cowboy.

Hamilton, John. *Rodeo Clown* (Xtreme Jobs). Minneapolis, MN: ABDO Publishing, 2015.
This book gives the history of rodeo clowning and how a rodeo clown is trained today. The job duties of a rodeo clown include entertaining the crowd with comedy routines and distracting bulls.

Harris, Lecile. *Lecile: This Ain't My First Rodeo.* Collierville, TN: Clowning Around Enterprises LLC, 2015.
Lecile Harris spent sixty years as a rodeo clown and still performs in over fifty rodeos annually. This book shares the experiences that he had over his career and gives insights into what this job is really like.

ORGANIZATIONS

National High School Rodeo Association
12011 Tejon Street, Suite 900
Denver, CO 80234
(800) 466-4772
Website: http://www.nhsra.com
This association is dedicated to promoting rodeo competition among high school students. It was organized in 1949 and since that time has sponsored rodeos all over the United States, Canada, and Australia.

Professional Rodeo Cowboys Association
101 Pro Rodeo Drive
Colorado Springs, CO 80919
(719) 528-4747
Website: http://prorodeo.com
This organization is the largest and oldest rodeo organization in the world. More than six hundred rodeos are sponsored by the association every year.

WEBSITES

Due to the changing nature of internet links, Rosen Publishing has developed an online list of websites related to the subject of this book. This site is updated regularly. Please use this link to access the list:

http://www.rosenlinks.com/CCWC/enter

CHAPTER 4

WORKING AS A CIRCUS PERFORMER

Running away to join the circus might seem like a pipe dream, but people actually do it! There are many different ways that people can make a living as circus performers. One is as a flying trapeze artist. Other circus jobs include contortionists, acrobats, jugglers, aerialists, tumblers, tight-rope walkers, and clowns. Circus performers may be employed to do just one of these jobs, or they might do several of them. Some requisite skills for a circus performer include:

- Develop basic acrobatic skills for certain circus jobs.
- Travel and live on the road while circuses are scheduled throughout the country
- Enjoy performing for people.
- Have basic hair, makeup, and costuming skills

Gymnasts make great circus performers—they have the acrobatic skills to perform many of the high-flying acts.

Flexibility and fearlessness is needed to perform high-flying stunts in the circus. Some professions in the circus, like that of this trapeze artist, require a high degree of practice and training to get to this level.

- Ability to get along with many different types of people—fellow performers, audience members, circus directors, and more.

All kinds of people join the circus. Some grew up in the circus themselves and then continued on with the family tradition. Others started out in other industries and found their way to the circus. Leah Christina Gonzalez, for example, started out as a gymnast and NFL cheerleader and ended up finding her way to the circus where she rides an elephant in the show. Some circus performers are immigrants from other countries who were trained in circuses in their native lands and then came to the United States as performers.

People who are attracted to circus entertaining are generally those who love to perform in front of an audience. They also must love to travel since the bulk of the year will be spent on the road. In addition, they must have very specific skills and talents. Not every job in the circus requires unique abilities, but many do.

PREPARING YOURSELF

College is absolutely not necessary for jobs in the circus. However, years of training in other ways are often necessary. Many circus performers are trained in gymnastics.

CIRCUS TRAINS

Ringling Bros. and Barnum & Bailey's circus generally uses train travel to move from one city to another. They have two trains, both of which have about sixty cars and are the longest privately owned trains in the world.

The circus trains house about 250 to 300 cast and crew members and their families year round. Families usually get half of a car to themselves. Many of these suites are bigger than New York City apartments. Set up just like houses, these cars have sleeping compartments, an eat-in kitchen, bathroom, and laundry facilities. Single people share a car with roommates, or "carmates." Each person gets his or her own room, but the bathroom facilities on those cars are shared. The cars have dedicated private spaces and also a centralized "pie car" where people can eat and socialize. Other cars on the train carry the sets, animals, and supplies for the circus. The train even carries automobiles for people to use at these stops. Since circuses are scheduled year round, the circus trains also provide school for children while their parents are working.

Ringmaster Jonathan Iverson travels with his family on the circus train. In a piece on Voice of America in 2012 he said, "It is so much fun. It gives us sort of like a mini-vacation every week. We really see the country. America is really, really beautiful." In the same article, Alex Barney, who is a second-generation clown with the circus, shared that "traveling by train is the key highlight for this job."

Circus announcers are crucial to a successful show. They may not perform the big stunts, but they definitely keep the audience alert and excited throughout the night.

They often start when they are young children. Flying trapeze and tight-rope walking are also very specific skills that must be taught in a school setting. Institutes like the American Youth Circus Organization are a great way to learn these skills. This particular school located in New York teaches all of the circus arts.

FUTURE PROSPECTS

There are two different categories of circus performers: those who work for big-name production companies (like Ringling Bros. or Cirque de Soleil) and those who are self-employed or freelance performers. Those who work for the production companies have a guaranteed income and other benefits like free housing (while they are on tour), health insurance, and retirement savings. Self-employed individuals have more freedom to work whatever jobs come their way, but they don't have the stability that a regular full-time production job provides.

FOR MORE INFORMATION

BOOKS

Franklin, Jill. *Beginners Guide to Aerial Silk*. Los Angeles, CA: Aerial Physique, 2014.
Franklin is the owner of a company that teaches aerial arts. This book gives step-by-step instructions on how to perform basic moves using aerial silk. It's presented as a supplement to qualified instruction.

Rooyackers, Paul. *101 Circus Games for Children: Juggling—Clowning—Balancing Acts—Acrobatics—Animal Numbers*. Hunter House, Amazon Digital Services LLC, 2012.
This book includes a variety of games that can be used for children's entertainment, including juggling, clowning, and acrobatics.

Simon, Linda. *Greatest Shows on Earth: A History of the Circus*. London, England: Reaktion Books, 2014.
This book details the history of circuses in the 1700s and concludes with modern-day circuses of today, including Cirque du Soleil.

ORGANIZATIONS

American Circus Educators (ACE)
PO Box 482
Ithaca, NY 14851
(914) 441-8834
Website: http://www.americancircuseducators.org
Formed in 2014, this organization supports circus educators with professional development, workshops, and classes. It also offers chances for circus teachers and coaches to network with each other.

American Youth Circus Organization
PO Box 482
Ithaca, NY 14851
(914) 441-8834
Website: http://www.americanyouthcircus.org
This organization was started to provide a place for youth to get involved in circus arts. It offers all kinds of classes, including acrobatics, aerial techniques, contortion, clowning, and juggling.

The Circus Project
1420 NW 17th Avenue, Suite 388
Portland, OR 97209
(503) 764-9174
Website: http://www.thecircusproject.org
This organization in Portland, Oregon is dedicated to contemporary circus arts education. All ages (adults and children) can take classes here in both recreational circus arts and pre-professional programs.

WEBSITES

Due to the changing nature of internet links, Rosen Publishing has developed an online list of websites related to the subject of this book. This site is updated regularly. Please use this link to access the list:

http://www.rosenlinks.com/CCWC/enter

CHAPTER 5

WORKING AS A CHILDREN'S ENTERTAINER

Imagine that you're dressed up like a clown entertaining children with balloons and games at a birthday party. The kids are laughing as you juggle fake oranges and do magic tricks with a toy rabbit stuffed into a top hat. Now, imagine that after this party, you immediately go out to your car, drive to the nearest restroom, switch into your gorilla costume with pink tutu, and then go deliver a birthday cake and balloons to a student at a high school. That night, you dress up once again in a frog costume and help out at a 5k race by high-fiving the children as they cross the finish line. The next morning, you grab

Balloon sculpting is a necessary skill for any children's entertainer to have in his or her arsenal of abilities. Performers must have patience and artistry to deal with and create for children, but successful entertainers find the work extremely rewarding.

your balloon collection and go to a restaurant where you tie balloon creatures for the children who are eating there with their families. Successful children's entertainers require the following:

- Enjoy working with children, while creating an entertaining environment
- Ability to transform into a variety of characters
- Dancing, theater, comedy, balloon twisting, ventriloquism, and musical training
- Marketing abilities to get the word out about who you are and what you offer (especially if you operate your own business)
- Travel, as many jobs require you to travel to onsite parties and events

All of these examples are what it would be like if you were employed as a children's entertainer. A person who has this job can find himself or herself working many different roles throughout their work week. That's especially true if the person works as a freelancer. However, if a person works for a company, they may only be contracted to work as a certain mascot, character, or princess and won't have to dress up in a bevy of different costumes. Children's entertainers at amusement parks, for example, will usually be hired to be just one character and will wear that costume every day.

People can make a career out of being a mascot or themed costumed character. The pay may not be great and the conditions might be challenging inside the costume, but the reward of seeing a child's face light up can make it all worth it.

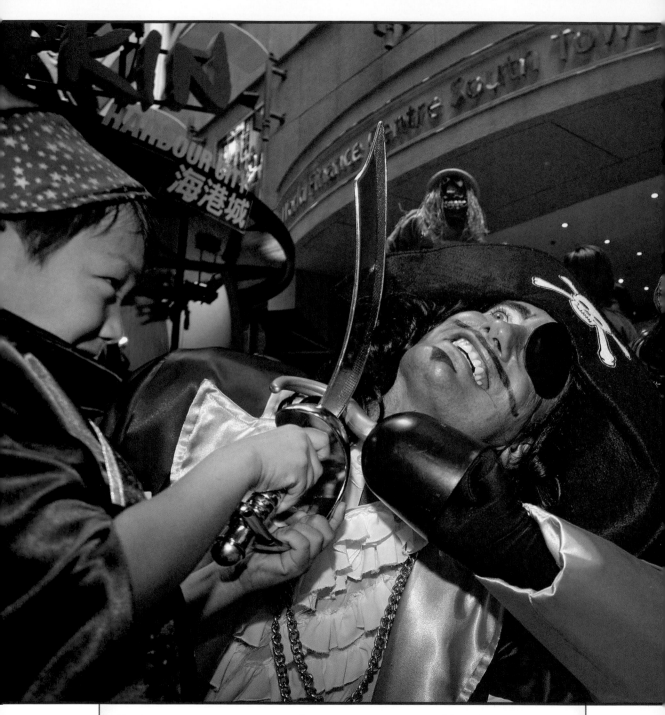

Putting on a costume can transform you into a variety of fun characters. You can go from being a bear mascot in the morning to a pirate in the evening!

There are numerous opportunities available for people who'd like to be a children's entertainer. You can work as a magician, ventriloquist, mime, balloon artist, princess, clown, juggler, mascot, Santa Claus, the Easter Bunny, and even the Grinch. The job locations are just as varied as the types of characters you could play. Children's entertainers are hired to perform at children's birthday parties at people's homes. They are hired to entertain at community events, hospital events, fund-raisers, church, school, and corporate events. Entertainers also perform at libraries, children's theaters, and museums. You can be hired to work at amusement parks and on cruise ships, too.

PREPARING YOURSELF

You do need some type of performance experience or have

INTERVIEW WITH EMILY REED, PARTY PRINCESS

According to Emily Reed, a professional party princess, her job is as thrilling as you'd expect. "Being a princess is pretty much as awesome as it sounds, especially if you're into the dress up and sing to little woodland animals kind of thing, which I very much am," says Reed. She entertains at children's birthday parties, contracted through a party company that organizes everything from scheduling to costumes and supplies. She loves the way the kids light up with excitement. "Being able to sing and act, which I absolutely love to do, and then have that make someone so happy is the perfect combination. I feel so blessed to be able to have a job that I love."

It's not all perfect joy in the princess business. There's a lot of travel involved, which Reed uses her own car for. Makeup, preparation, and travel take up an enormous amount of time. Reed says she occasionally spends far more time preparing for the gig than actually entertaining. The best way to prepare, says this professional princess, is to get familiar with the characters you can play. Develop skills you can use, like learning how to do bold makeup with contouring and fake lashes. Learning how to face paint for parties and do balloon twists are a big plus. You'll also get paid more if you have your own costumes and supplies.

the desire and willingness to be taught the basics. You can learn these basics in high school drama classes, community theater, private acting classes, and by apprenticing with other children's entertainers.

In addition to training, you also must have a certain personality and temperament for this job. Most importantly: you need to like being around children. You certainly won't make it very long as a children's entertainer if you are only working for the money. You must also have a fun, easy-going, and carefree personality. You should also like to dress up in costumes, as many of the characters you portray will be costumed ones.

Having initiative and a good work ethic is also important for this type of job. Some people will work for an agency or party company, but others will be freelancers and have to find their own work. If you are the latter, then you certainly can't just sit around and wait for the jobs to come your way—at least not at first. You have to market yourself, your brand, and your company so that people know they should call you for their children's events. If you are a freelancer, you may want to take some business workshops or read books on how to best run your freelance children's entertainment business.

FUTURE PROSPECTS

As long as there are children on this earth, there will be a need for children's entertainers! This job field is so vast that job seekers can find many different types of opportunities if they are willing to be creative in their approach. Remember: in order to make a living at this job, you must be flexible in the types of roles you're willing to play. If you market yourself as Santa Claus during the holidays, for example, don't expect that you'll be able to make a living all year long with that one costume. You'll have to have other characters in your entertainment arsenal to use during the other eleven months of the year.

FOR MORE INFORMATION

BOOKS

Gallagher, M. J. *Let's Make a Scene!* Mighty Gargoyle Media, Amazon Digital Services LLC, 2014.
This book has a selection of unique plays for children's theater including "Cindy Claus Saves Christmas," "Fast Times at Holiday High," and "One Lucky Night."

Pincus, Wendy. *How To Make Popular Balloon Animals for Parties.* Amazon Digital Services LLC, 2015.
In this book, Pincus provides step-by-step instructions for how to create the most commonly requested balloon animals.

Shearing, Linda. *Kids' Party Planner! Children's Party Planning Made Quick And Easy!* Amazon Digital Services LLC, 2014.
While children's entertainers usually show up and don't necessarily have to plan the actual party, sometimes they are asked to plan the event. On those occasions, this particular book is very helpful in figuring out all of the necessary steps for a successful soiree.

ORGANIZATIONS

International Jugglers Association
Website: http://dev.juggle.org
This mostly volunteer organization provides jugglers around the world of all ages a place to communicate and compete. Started in 1947, its mission is to preserve the art of juggling for future generations.

KIDabra International
PO Box 1296
Mocksville, NC 27028
(336) 492-7870
Website: http://www.kidabra.org
This organization is for family entertainers to meet, share ideas, and provide support for each other. The annual KIDabra conference provides workshops and gives entertainers a chance to network with each other.

Kids Entertainer Hub (KEH)
264 Manchester Road, 1st Floor
Warrington, Cheshire WA1 3RB
England
Website: http://kidsentertainerhub.com

Started by two kids entertainers who wanted a way to network with other people in their industry, KEH is a digital space where entertainers around the world can meet, discuss, brainstorm, and collaborate.

WEBSITES

Due to the changing nature of internet links, Rosen Publishing has developed an online list of websites related to the subject of this book. This site is updated regularly. Please use this link to access the list:

http://www.rosenlinks.com/CCWC/enter

CHAPTER 6

WORKING AS A DANCER

Dance is not only a beautiful visual art form, it is also a very diverse one. There are many genres of dance that can be learned and performed professionally including hip-hop, ballet, modern dance, tap, ballroom, folk dance, hula, country western dance, Latin dancing, belly dancing, breakdancing, clogging, Irish river dancing, yoga, and Zumba.

Those pursuing a career in dance will need to develop other skills besides the ability to dance. They must have creativity, athleticism, and the willingness to work as a member of a team. Dancers also need to be resourceful when it comes to finding work, not only as a dancer but also to supplement their dance income. Dancing gigs don't always pay the bills, so dancers will often

Dancers have a better chance finding work in big entertainment markets like Los Angeles and New York City.

have to find side jobs like serving at restaurants, working in retail, or teaching dance in private studios, community centers, or at gyms to make extra money. When pursuing dance as a career, some important considerations are:

- Advanced dance training
- Continued physical fitness required as this is a very active profession
- Ability to memorize dance steps and routines
- Marketing skills, either as a business owner or to get the word out in the business about who you are
- Travel, since some dance jobs require touring

It's important to note that teaching doesn't have to be considered a way to make supplemental income. Rather it can be viewed as a chosen career path of its own. Dance instructors can make a good living by teaching or coaching others. Some work freelance and travel from place to place to teach classes. Instructors can work as part of an established large studio and get paid an hourly rate. Others choose to open their own dance studio either in their home or in a rented space. That's what Nesha Woodhouse did in 2000 when she started her own dance studio in the basement of her house. Eventually, the studio became so popular that she hired a staff of nineteen instructors and constructed a building to house her studio.

Dancers often spend hours every day honing their skills. They often begin young, too, around the age of 3 or 4. But there are many forms of dance, and many ways to start, so the best thing to do is get involved now!

PRO CHEERLEADING, IS IT REALLY AS IT APPEARS?

The life of a professional cheerleader looks glamorous, dressing up in cute costumes, wearing beautiful makeup, and having a perfect tan. But according to some recent lawsuits by NFL cheerleaders in 2015 and 2016, cheerleading is a less-than-perfect gig. Cheerleaders have traditionally received very low pay. They receive a small amount per game (like $125 dollars), generally received at the end of the season. They are not paid for practice times, public appearances, or other team-related events that they are required to attend. For the hours they work, the hourly pay is well below minimum wage. Cheerleaders are expected to stay in perfect shape during the season and keep up on all their dance routines. Frequent weigh-ins make sure they haven't gained any weight. If they have, they must sit in the locker room (unpaid) during that game. Most teams also require that cheerleaders have flawless tans during the season, which the cheerleaders attain either by spray tanning or visiting a tanning bed. Some of these requirements (the strict weight limit and the tanning) could cause health problems for the cheerleaders later in life.

Many cheerleaders are unhappy with the way they're being treated. Some of the teams have already settled with the cheerleaders out of court. California judges ordered that cheerleaders start to be treated like employees instead of independent contractors. But it's only fair to also point out that while some cheerleaders are unhappy, others are not. One cheerleader anonymously told the *Independent Journal Review* in 2016, "One of the things that was made *very clear* before I became a cheerleader were the time commitments and compensation. Even before tryouts, I knew what to expect."

It might seem glamorous to be a professional cheerleader, but there's more to the job than meets the eye.

PREPARING YOURSELF

Most dancers begin taking dance instruction at a very early age, sometimes even as young as three or four years old. Training is pretty basic during childhood and becomes more intense during the preteen years. For more classical

Dancers can also make a living by becoming either a teacher or a choreographer, or a combination of the two. Often professional dancers become teachers when they stop dancing full time.

studies like ballet, intense instruction at a professional dance studio is a necessity, especially if the ballerina wants to go on to perform at big-name companies later on. But students can also obtain a significant amount of dance training by taking dance in high school. Dance classes are part of the art and physical education programs. Also, there are groups such as drill team and cheerleading that are made up of dancers, too. Summer dance camps, which include specialized instruction and competitions, are another way that dancers can obtain dance training during their teenage years. After high school, some dancers go on to major in dance in college, but that is not required in order to pursue a career in dance.

FUTURE PROSPECTS

Between 2014 and 2024, jobs for dancers and choreographers are expected to increase by 5 percent according to the US Bureau of Labor Statistics. That is about the same expected growth rate as most other occupations. The jobs will most likely be found at small companies and dance competition companies rather than at large companies. Besides getting a job at a dance company, dancers and choreographers can also look for work at theme parks and in music videos, as well as in movies, television, or on online video sites like YouTube. They can also be dance teachers who teach in their own private studios or at gyms. Be forewarned, there is stiff competition for available jobs in the dance world. So, be prepared to work hard and be persistent if you want to have a career in this industry.

FOR MORE INFORMATION

BOOKS

Colton, Sandra. *Book Me! How to Become a Successful Working Dancer in Hollywood.* Los Angeles, CA: Pinstriped Publishing, 2012.
Colton gives specific instructions on how to make it as a dancer in Hollywood. She gives tips and tricks based on experiences and stories from more than one hundred working dancers and choreographers.

Dagenais, Mande. *Starting Your Career as a Dancer.* New York, NY: Allworth Press, 2012.
This book tells how to get into and thrive in the business of dancing. The author uses her twenty-five years of experience as a dancer, teacher, choreographer/director, and producer to advise in the book.

Shaffer, Matthew. *So You Want to Be a Dancer: Practical Advice and True Stories from a Working Professional.* Lanham, MD: Taylor Trade Publishing, 2015.
Shafer gleans from his twenty years of performing to share what it takes to become a successful dancer. He details how to break into the industry with specific auditioning and job-seeking techniques.

ORGANIZATIONS

National Dance Council of America (NDCA)
PO Box 22018
Provo, UT 84602
(801) 422-81242
Website: http://www.ndca.org
NDCA is the official governing council of dance in
the USA. It represents the interests of all dance-
related activities, including competitor information,
educational opportunities, and events.

National Dance Education Organization
8609 Second Avenue, Suite #203-B
Silver Spring, MD 20910
(301) 585-2880
Website: http://www.ndeo.org
This organization is dedicated to advancing dance
education in the arts. Professional development, online
education, research, and advocacy are all included in
the structure of the organization.

WEBSITES

Due to the changing nature of internet links, Rosen Publishing has developed an online list of websites related to the subject of this book. This site is updated regularly. Please use this link to access the list:

http://www.rosenlinks.com/CCWC/enter

CHAPTER 7

WORKING AS A PUPPETEER

A puppeteer is a person who brings inanimate objects to life. Puppeteers have been entertaining since ancient times. Many children's programs on television use puppetry, including *Sesame Street, Bear in the Big Blue House,* and *The Muppets.* Puppets are even found in action movies, like the aliens in *Men in Black.* Puppeteers and their puppets were also used in the filming of the 2016 blockbuster remake of *The Jungle Book.*

There are all kinds of puppeteers. Some make their own puppets out of metal and papier-mâché or decorate socks and use them for hand puppets. Others use marionettes and some work with life-size or larger puppets and animatronics. Many puppeteers can find jobs in theaters, studios (television and film), amusement parks, and as independent performers through:

- Natural or developed storytelling skills.
- The ability to write stories and plays so performances are unique.

For more than 50 years, there has been a puppet festival in Charleville-Mezieres, France.

- Marketing abilities: many puppeteers are entrepreneurs, and those who are not still need to get their name out in the business in order to get hired for jobs.
- Attend ventriloquist training courses to develop those skills.
- Learn how to make your own puppets, or find reputable sources to purchase them.
- Enjoy entertaining children.

One of the challenges to a career in puppetry is that puppeteers sometimes have to work in awkward spaces. They'll have to crouch below the set so they're not seen by the audience. They'll have to be contorted into uncomfortable positions behind the scenes. They'll have to spend large amounts of time inside hot, furry costumes. However, there are many benefits to a job in this career, too. For one, you get to pretend to be funny and lovable characters. You get to take on the role of many characters at once and use a variety of voices to play the scene. Not many people get to be every character in a play, and a puppeteer often has that opportunity.

Puppeteers have many responsibilities. First, if they are on the stage with their puppets instead of hiding behind the set, they have to decide if they are going to use ventriloquism when they perform their puppets' parts. If they decide to do so, this is a challenging skill that can take a lot of time (and

Not all puppets are cuddly. Often they are a masterful work of art. Some, like this one, have a more alien appearance.

INTERVIEW WITH LISA LAIRD, PUPPETEER AND VENTRILOQUIST

Puppeteer Lisa Laird uses ventriloquism, puppetry, magic, and storytelling in her programs. She explains, "The storytelling aspects of my show are sometimes in conjunction with puppets, sometimes with magic and sometimes with other props or costumes." Laird learned ventriloquism through the Maher Ventriloquism course and also took other classes and private training from professional ventriloquists. She also attends conferences and continuing education to keep on top of new skills. Laird loves working with kids and telling stories.

If you're interested in puppetry, Laird recommends participating in drama and speech in high school to get comfortable with performance and the process of what it takes to put a show together. Seeking out resources such as Puppeteers of America and watching as many puppetry performances as possible will introduce you to a wide range of styles and performances. Some puppeteers or theaters will even take on apprentices to teach the trade.

practice) to master. Puppeteers also frequently write their own scripts and plays. Puppeteers are generally people who have a good sense of humor. They often incorporate funny elements, slapstick-style comedy, and bits of irony into their sketches. After all, one of the main purposes of puppetry is to make the audience happy and help them have an enjoyable time.

PREPARING YOURSELF

There are some formal education opportunities for puppetry, but that is certainly not necessary. Most people learn puppetry by working with a skilled puppeteer. Many puppeteers attend classes on the university level after they have already been in the business for years, in order to gain additional skills. They might also take a workshop or two in order to learn more difficult techniques (like ventriloquism).

FUTURE PROSPECTS

Most puppeteers are self-employed, or work on a freelance basis. Because of that, there are many options for employment opportunities. You will not be looking around for the next available job to come up. Instead, you can start your own theater, and through hard work, good marketing strategies,

Avenue Q was a Broadway show that primarily featured puppets.

and willingness to put in a lot of hours preparing and performing, you can make a successful business for yourself. Marketing strategies can (and should) include using social media, setting up a business website, and networking with teachers, librarians, museum employees, and people who operate festivals. You can volunteer your skills at hospitals, children's centers, and other facilities. You can also turn your skills to the online world by videoing your performances and creating your own YouTube channel. This can be a source of revenue by itself once you get enough hits. It can also be a portfolio builder. You can share these videos on your business website as well and use them for promotional materials for future clients.

FOR MORE INFORMATION

BOOKS

Bryan, Ashley. *Ashley Bryan's Puppets: Making Something from Everything*. New York, NY: Atheneum, 2014.
This book tells of an African storyteller who makes puppets out of found objects on the beaches near his home. It includes photos of the puppets and accompanying poems that describe how they were made.

Hunt, Deborah. *Puppets, Puppetry, and Gogmagog: A Manual for Constructing Puppets*. San Juan, PR: Maskhunt Motions, 2013.
The author has worked for more than thirty-five years as a puppeteer. She uses puppets and other objects in her performances. This book teaches readers how to create twenty-four different styles of puppets to use for all kinds of performances.

Mason, Taylor. *The Complete Idiot's Guide to Ventriloquism*. New York, NY: Alpha, 2012.
This book is designed for the beginner who wants to learn the basics of ventriloquism. It provides a brief history of the skill, gives guidelines of basic ventriloquist techniques, and tells how to buy a "dummy."

ORGANIZATIONS
Center for Puppetry Arts
1404 Spring Street, NW
Atlanta, GA 30309
(404) 873-3391
Website: http://www.centerforpuppetryarts.com
The purpose of this organization is to "inspire imagination, education and community through the global art of puppetry." Both children and adults can be educated and entertained through the art of puppetry.

Puppeteers of America
Sabathani Community Center
310 East 38th Street, Suite 127
Minneapolis, MN 55409
(612) 821-2382
Website: https://www.puppeteers.org
This national nonprofit organization promotes puppetry around the nation. The organization has produced more than 160 national and regional puppetry festivals over the years.

International Ventriloquist Society
341 Papaya Circle
Barefoot Bay, FL 32976
Website: http://maherstudios.com
This society offers mentorship and training in the art of ventriloquism. It also provides information on job markets, how to design a show, scriptwriting techniques, and an annual convention.

VIDEOS

White, Amy, Mark Pulham, and Dallin Blankenship. *Dressing the Naked Hand (Book + DVD): The World's Greatest Guide to Making, Staging, and Performing with Puppets.* Sanger, CA: Familius, 2015.
This DVD provides hours of instruction on how to make, stage, and perform with puppets. It is accompanied by a 184-page book.

WEBSITES

Due to the changing nature of internet links, Rosen Publishing has developed an online list of Web sites related to the subject of this book. This site is updated regularly. Please use this link to access the list:

http://www.rosenlinks.com/CCWC/enter

CHAPTER 8

WORKING IN SET CONSTRUCTION AND STAGE CREWING

In stage and screen productions, the set is a very integral part of the performance. Imagine a scene where two characters are sitting on a couch in a living room. It's a simple scene with simple dialogue—maybe just a few lines or so. But the set isn't at all simple. This is a fake house built specifically for this scene. Someone had to build that house from the ground up. Then, someone else had to choose the furniture, wall décor, carpeting, paint colors, and so forth. The setting of a scene tells about the characters (their wealth, or lack of), the time period, the time of year, and the time of day. It takes an entire crew of people working behind the scenes to make all of

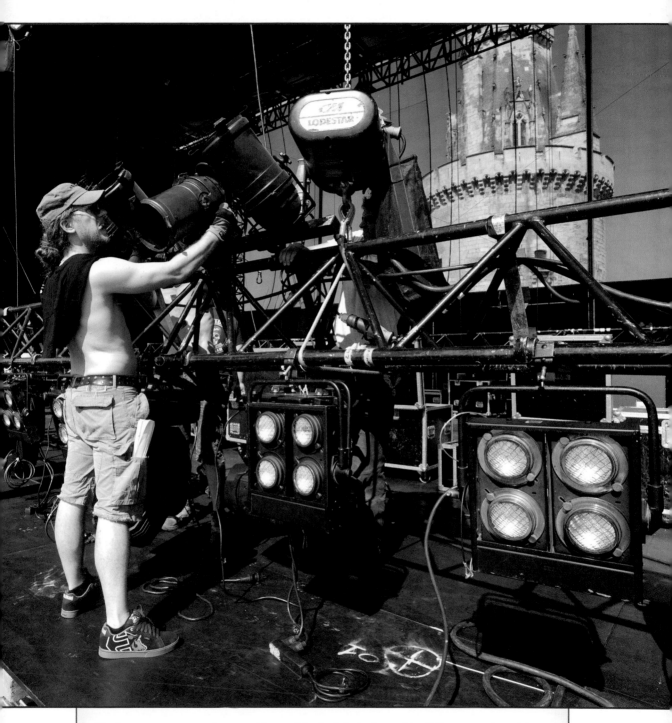

Tech crews must enjoy working with their hands and building creative things that will likely be torn down once the performance is over.

this happen. These folks are the stage crew, set designers, and scenery movers, artists, builders, and constructors. The behind-the-scenes professionals are also people who work on lighting, sound, and the placement of props. Behind-the-scenes pros are needed in all kinds of performances. These people work in any place that has a stage or a set: television, theme parks, theater, circuses, dance performances, large and small concerts, and cruise ships. Some requirements for crewmembers include:

- Technical and construction skills, or be willing to learn them
- Proficiency in specific trade skills like electrical work, lighting, carpentry, and heavy equipment
- Think outside the box—many jobs require improvisation in order to get equipment to work just right
- Work long hours away from a nine-to-five schedule
- Travel, as some jobs require settting up in touring locations
- Physical strength—many jobs require physical labor and little sleep during peak production times

Simon Lovelace, the founder of a technical crew company, explained in an article on Guardian.com that jobs in this career field are certainly not glamorous. He says that instead of going to after-parties to celebrate an amazing performance or concert, the stage people are usually still on-set breaking

Setting up the lights is an important part of a concert. This man is part of the stage crew at the Francofiles music festival in La Rochelle, Montreal.

everything down. The job often requires lots of hard physical labor and little sleep during peak production times. Yet, in life and in stage work, lots of sweat and tears can also bring forth great rewards. Lovelace says, "If you're working on a big music or theater tour—even if you're the lowest, humblest scaffolder—and you turn up in an empty field and two weeks later you've built Glastonbury, you stand back and say 'we did that.'"

Work on cruise ships can be both challenging and exciting. Take for example the rock cruises that allow fans to attend a cruise with their favorite bands. Stage crews will be responsible for everything related to the concerts. If a concert is scheduled for an island port, then the crew will need to go ahead of time to set up the stage and sound equipment so that it's all ready when the band and passengers arrive. Stage crew managers will also be responsible for doing whatever is necessary to make the band happy. The responsibilities of the back-stage crews are definitely both interesting and extensive.

Keeping up-to-date on theater technology is a crucial part of this business. The skills learned in shop class or constructing and staging sets for a high school production can provide a valuable starting point for a student interested in theater tech and construction.

PREPARING YOURSELF

Stage work requires proficiency in specific trade skills like electrical work, lighting, carpentry, and heavy equipment (booms, lifts, forklifts, backhoes, and front loaders) operating. For that type of specific work, a stage person must generally come to the job already knowing those skills. These particular skills are often attained through apprenticeships and other work opportunities. Other less-technical jobs (like helping place props on a set) take little to no background experience. You are merely trained on the set while working. Set designers might have backgrounds in interior design, but they also might just be trained in an apprenticeship or internship.

Certain organizations and institutes also provide training for their members in all kinds of theater technology. This is especially important since technology continues to change and improve all the time. Even people who have been in the industry for a while may still need to take these classes in order to stay up on the latest equipment that they'll be required to use in their jobs. The United States Institute for Theater Technology is one such organization with extensive training available for people in stage work.

INTERVIEW WITH JEFF BLOOM, STAGE AND SET CONSTRUCTION

Live show specialist Jeff Bloom is a rigger, carpenter/grip, and fork lift operator and sometimes a lighting electrician and welder/set builder. He covers concerts, award shows, plays, musicals, operas, dance performances, and some television, like *Dancing With the Stars* and *American Idol*. His typical rigging day for concerts includes unloading trucks, laying-out and hanging all rig points (audio, video, lighting, and anything else that needs to go in the air), and tweaking all of these points as requested. This is always done with a whole team of workers. For example, for a recent Justin Bieber concert, he had to rig a twenty-foot-by-sixty-foot (six-meter-by-eighteen-meter) trampoline to fly onto the stage and then fly back out after two songs. It was a challenge! There were around forty people who worked on that particular job. Once a concert is over, the crew has to come back to reverse the process. The pay is good, and there are always fresh challenges. But it can be stressful to not have a set nine-to-five schedule and also not know when you will or will not have work.

Bloom's advice to young people interested in this industry is " just get out there and do it." Take the money you make and take any specialized classes you might be interested in like rope access, ETCP, and lighting/sound board operation to build your skills. He also recommends that if you are going to be on the labor force, you should join a union, which adds benefits, stability, and advancement.

FUTURE PROSPECTS

Jobs for actors are expected to increase between 2014 and 2024, according to the US Department of Labor. Where there are jobs for actors, there are also jobs for set crews. Even on professional-level online videos, set people are still needed. According to information found on Recruiter.com, careers in the set or exhibit design field are expected to increase by 7.07 percent by 2018. There are also more jobs found in this industry in the states of California and New York than in any other state. That's no surprise considering that's where Hollywood and Broadway, respectively, are located.

FOR MORE INFORMATION

BOOKS

Brewster, Karen, and Melissa Shafer. *Fundamentals of Theatrical Design: A Guide to the Basics of Scenic, Costume, and Lighting Design*. New York, NY: Allworth Press, 2011.
Brewster and Shafer provide details on how scenery, costumes, and lighting are linked. This book is a great reference for people who work behind-the-scenes on sets and stage crew.

Kaluta, John. *The Perfect Stage Crew: The Complete Technical Guide for High School, College, and Community Theater*. New York, NY: Allworth Press, 2016.
This public high school teacher shares his stage experience putting on shows over the last twenty-five years. He's worked installing television studio equipment, operating pyrotechnics, and designing lighting and sets.

Lord, Rick M. *A Gaffer's Perspective on Independent Filmmaking: Practices, Techniques and Tricks of The Trade Revealed*. Boca Raton, FL: Universal Publishers, 2011
In this book a gaffer (lighting expert) tells his experience in independent filmmaking and how indie films can improve by using techniques from Hollywood productions.

ORGANIZATIONS

Set Decorators Society of America (SDSA)
7100 Tujunga Avenue, Suite #A
North Hollywood, CA 91605
(818) 255-2425
Website: http://www.setdecorators.org
This organization represents design teams for films, television, and commercials. Its mission is to promote a high standard of excellence and preserve the legacy of set decoration in movies and television.

Stage Managers' Association (SMA)
PO Box 526, Times Square Station
New York, NY 10108
Website: http://www.stagemanagers.org
This professional organization for stage managers aims to create a network. This supportive environment is designed to help all stage managers improve in their careers.

United States Institute for Theater Technology (USITT)
315 S Crouse Avenue, Suite 200
Syracuse, NY 13210
(800) 938-7488
Website: http://www.usitt.org
USITT provides training programs for people interested in all aspects of theater technology. The organization also provides seminars, mentoring, and networking opportunities for its members.

VIDEOS

"Stage Technician: Job Profile"
https://www.youtube.com/watch?v=U69JrFLtKXc
This YouTube video features an interview with a stage technician in Scotland. He answers questions about what his job entails and what advice he has for budding stage technicians.

WEBSITES

Due to the changing nature of internet links, Rosen Publishing has developed an online list of websites related to the subject of this book. This site is updated regularly. Please use this link to access the list:

http://www.rosenlinks.com/CCWC/enter

CHAPTER 9

WORKING AS A VOICEOVER ACTOR

Voice actors provide the voices for amusement parks, commercials, animation, games, public service announcements, trailers, company videos, online promotions, nonfiction documentaries, television shows, and movies. According to voice actor Beau Stephenson in an article for the *Los Angeles Times* in 2015, his first job was doing voiceover work for a real estate software company's training video. This gave him a portfolio piece and networking contacts, which led to more opportunities, including video game trailers, health club commercials, and projects with big-name production companies. The voiceover acting business has been part of entertainment ever since sound was used in radio. Walt Disney is considered a pioneer in voiceover for film—beginning in 1928, he was the voice actor for the Mickey Mouse character in the animation "Steamboat Willie."

Voice actors need a special set of skills for their work:

- Training in voice or dialect (from a coach or theater professional)
- Marketing skills to put forward your reputation and seek work
- Positive, stick-with-it attitude—you will not get most of the jobs you audition for
- Comfort in a solitary environment, as most work is completed in a home studio
- Technical skills to operate a computer, sound system, and microphone

In the past, voice actors had to travel from studio to studio to get work. Or, they just worked in-house with a production company. However, today many voice actors work from home studios, but they still might be required to come into a production studio on occasion. This is why it's important to live in an area where voice acting is in highest demand. As far as a home studio is concerned, these can be built easily

Acting classes are helpful in getting the right diction and sound out of your voice.

Sports announcers must have a certain sound to their voices (and a knowledge of the sport) in order to be successful in the business. Many start by working with their high school sports teams.

with a couple of thousand dollars in investment. Stephenson built his own sound studio out of wood and carpet that he purchased at a local hardware store. Then, to complete the studio, he set up his electronic equipment: a computer with the latest mixing software, a microphone, a sound mixer, and an internet connection.

PREPARING YOURSELF

In an interview with the author, voice actor Liz Abbott provided advice on ways to prepare for a voiceover (VO) career. She suggests looking online to research different types of VO work, listen to top voice talent demos, and learning about industry trends. Understanding how to market yourself is also crucial, as success often comes more from marketing than from innate talent. The best way to build your skills is to begin taking lessons in acting, singing, and speech/dialects. It's also important to work with a VO coach. Coaches are listed in the Voice Over Resource Guide, an online resource. Be sure to research a coach's credentials. Many coaches work via Skype, so you do not need to be located near them. It's also necessary to become comfortable with technology, as you'll likely be recording and editing from home. Keep in mind that your voice will not be right for every role. You must develop a thick skin and not take it personally when your audition is not selected. It's just business, and there will always be more opportunities.

FUTURE PROSPECTS

The entertainment industry is booming. The US Department of Labor anticipates that actors will see a 10 percent increase in jobs between 2014 and 2024. Jobs are increasing in television, movies, on-demand movies, and online videos. Voiceover is also experiencing an increase as well. However, keep in mind that just like in other areas of acting, the competition is stiff. In order to be marketable in the industry, notes Liz Abbott, you need professional-sounding voice demo recordings to showcase your abilities, and you should be available to clients during regular business hours. If you must work a part-time job when you're starting out, that job will need to be in off-hours so it won't interfere with VO opportunities

Even though you perform alone in a studio, you should act as though you're performing for a live audience. This helps to animate your performance.

INTERVIEW WITH VOICEOVER ACTOR LIZ ABBOTT

Liz Abbott has several agents, but finds much of her work herself. Her favorite projects are ones where she gets to play with her voice in character roles. The best part of her job, says Abbott, is the flexibility of the casting available. "A little boy? A puppy? An elf? No one would cast me in those roles based on my age or how I look, but with VO there are tons of possibilities!" While character voices are fun, the majority of available VO work is narration and commercial. Some voice actors specialize in one or two areas while others are more diverse. One possible downside of a VO career is isolation. Abbott explains: "I work with clients remotely via email, phone, or Skype each day, but I don't have co-workers that I see on a regular basis."

A typical day for Liz starts with vocal warm-ups followed by time recording jobs and auditions. Then she edits and sends sound files. She also spends time finding, emailing, and cold calling potential clients. Later she might work with a coach or watch online interviews with VO casting directors. Liz loves the freedom of planning her own schedule but admits freelancing can be stressful as it lacks the predictable benefits of a salaried position.

that can come in at the last minute. Explains Abbott: "It's advantageous to be one of the first to submit an audition. Also many clients will want the job recorded and edited within a couple of hours, and some will want to listen in and direct while you record. If you're at another job elsewhere, this will not be possible and you will lose the opportunity." When you're just starting, a home studio anywhere will do, as most work is done remotely. You can find online tutorials to help optimize a home VO studio. As you progress in your career, you may consider moving to a larger market such as Los Angeles or New York.

FOR MORE INFORMATION

BOOKS

Courvoisier, Dave. *More Than Just a Voice: The REAL Secret to VoiceOver Success.* Amazon Digital Services LLC, 2014.

Courvoisier's approach is to help actors be prepared for these jobs and find these jobs—all while utilizing his decades of experience in the voice-acting business.

McClanaghan, Kate. *How To Get More Voice Acting Jobs: Marketing 101 for Actors & Voiceovers.* Book Baby, Amazon Digital Services LLC, 2013.

The author details how to find jobs and how to prepare your portfolio work using equipment in your own home and how to be personally engaged in finding work and not leave it "up to" an agent.

Roers, Natalie. *How to Become a Voice Over Artist: Make a Living from Home with your Voice!* Amazon Digital Services LLC, 2014.

This book offers a step-by-step guide to making a living at home doing voiceover work. An industry veteran, the author explains her process, how she found work, and how she set up her own studio.

Strikwerda, Paul. *Making Money In Your PJs: Freelancing for Voice-Overs and Other Solopreneurs*. Nethervoice Publishing, Amazon Digital Services LLC, 2014. Strikwerda is a veteran voiceover actor. He emphasizes helping those interested in the career to be successful by treating voiceover acting as a career and not as a hobby.

ORGANIZATIONS

Voiceover Universe
Website: http://www.voiceoveruniverse.com
This organization allows voiceover actors around the world to connect and share industry news. The website offers blogs, videos, events, gigs, audition information, and other related voiceover resources.

Voices
25 Broadway, 9th floor
New York, NY 10004
(888) 359-3472
Website: https://www.voices.com

Voices provides opportunities for voiceover talent to find jobs and people looking for voiceover work to find talent. Voices was founded by David and Stephanie Ciccarelli in 2003.

World-Voices Organization
Website: http://www.world-voices.org
This is a group of international freelance voiceover actors who educate, promote, and encourage others in the industry. A small membership fee is required to join the group.

VIDEOS

Voiceover Artist Animation Voice Actor David Kaye
https://www.youtube.com/watch?v=QWsY3aTnyaM
In this video, Burbank-based voiceover actor David Kaye explains what it's like to be in the business. He gives advice to budding voiceover actors about how they can best make it in the business.

WEBSITES

Due to the changing nature of internet links, Rosen Publishing has developed an online list of websites related to the subject of this book. This site is updated regularly. Please use this link to access the list:

http://www.rosenlinks.com/CCWC/enter

CHAPTER 10

WORKING AS A FOLEY ARTIST

Have you ever thought about all of the sounds that a movie, television show, commercial, or radio program contains? Even in a relatively quiet scene, you can still hear a person walking down a hallway, the wind rustling through the trees, and a person struggling to get his umbrella down during a rainstorm. These sounds don't just happen during the filming. Well, they might happen, but they aren't going to be very distinct in the filming of the scene. Many of the sounds (other than dialogue and music) that are heard in a filmed production were most likely re-created during postproduction by a special artist called a Foley artist. Foley art was named after the pioneer sound artist Jack Foley (1891–1967) who created sound effects in film in the 1930s. Today, Foley artists depend on a variety of skills:

You'd be surprised at the types of props used to make the sounds you hear on films, television, and commercials. They often come from unexpect places!

Want the sound of galloping horses? Then use a pair of coconuts attached to wooden poles. Being a Foley artist is all about creative use of props, sound, and audio effects to produce what an audience expects to hear while they watch a film. Foley artists enhance, rather than distract, from the action on screen.

- Ability to think outside the box—the majority of the work will consist of making sounds that come from unexpected sources
- Networking skills to get your name known in the business
- Fun, creative personality
- Training from other professionals in the field on an apprentice basis

There are three main types of sound effects that Foley artists re-create. The first are called "clothes tracks." These are any sounds that an individual's clothes make in the film. This could be the sound of someone's purse brushing up against their body or the sound of ski pants rubbing together as a skier swooshes down the slopes. The second type of sound effects are called "footstep tracks," which is the sound that a person or animal makes while walking or running. The third are called "prop tracks," which are the sounds that various objects in the film might make. The Foley artist re-creates these sounds by watching the film reel and then re-creating the sound that should be made during each bit of scene.

PREPARING YOURSELF

There are no schools that teach Foley art. The majority of people learn on the job or as apprentices. For film work, most jobs are found in Los Angeles, since that's where the big Hollywood production companies are located. It's highly recommended that if you want to become a Foley artist in film that you relocate to Los Angeles. When you're there, networking is the best way to find opportunities for apprenticeships. Use social media to connect with others in the business, and ask your friends if they know any Foley artists and, if so, they'll introduce you. Visit audio postproduction offices or sound studios and offer to work

Foley artists collect their own "prop bags" and will take those items with them to studio assignments when needed. An artist is only as good as the tools they have on hand.

THE FOLEY STAGE

The magic of Foley work happens on the Foley stage or studio. This is where the artist has all of the equipment and supplies that are used to make various types of sounds. A Foley stage could be confused for a huge garage sale! A key element of a Foley stage is what is sometimes called the "props store." You'll find all kinds of things here like old bicycles, furniture, appliances, pots, pans, clothing, shoes, the crunched hood of an old car, a mini-swimming pool, food products, and different types of floor surfaces. Anything can essentially be turned into a Foley prop.

The best thing about Foley work is that your creativity and imagination are constantly being used to figure out how to re-create sounds in a film. You will rarely use the exact same object that is used in the film. "The real movement doesn't sound as real as you'd want it to and the [Foley] artist must find a more suitable object with which to create the sound," explains Foley artist Tony Eckert in an article on Filmsound. org. For example, if you were trying to re-create the sound that a dog makes as it walks across a wood floor, you wouldn't have a dog walk across a wood floor! That will not reliably make the same sound as what the film is depicting. Instead, you would find something else to use for the sound. One Foley artist accomplished this by taking a pair of gloves, taping paper clips on the ends of the fingers to represent the claws, and then using those to tap out the exact rhythm of the dog's movements.

for free as an intern or runner. Do an internet search for "Foley artists," "film sound," "sound effects," and other similar searches to find the most current resources. Even seasoned master Foley artists will continue to hone their craft and try to find new ways to make sounds feel more realistic.

FUTURE PROSPECTS

Entertainment isn't going anywhere. Hollywood movies and television shows are expected to increase in number by 2024. The US Bureau of Labor Statistics predicts there will be an increased need by 10 percent for actors from 2014 to 2024. With that increased need, it's safe to also assume that there will be an increased need for Foley artists as well. Granted, there are some sound effects that can be made using digital processes without the need for human interaction with props. However, there are an even higher number of sound effects that need the human involvement in order to make the sounds as realistic as possible. The only trick will be finding someone to train you and finding work. Remember: network, network, network! That is the real key to finding jobs in this particular field.

FOR MORE INFORMATION

BOOKS

Ament, Vanessa Theme. *The Foley Grail: The Art of Performing Sound for Film, Games, and Animation, Second Edition.* Burlington, MA: Focal Press, 2014.
In this book, Ament explains the basic to advanced methods of Foley art that are used in films, broadcast, animation, and games.

Owens, Jim, and Gerald Millerson. *Television Production.* Burlington, MA: Focal Press, 2012.
Owens and Millerson explore all aspects of television production in this extensive 456-page book. It uses the expertise of these authors as veterans in the television industry for more than thirty years.

Schenk, Sonja. *The Digital Filmmaking Handbook.* Independence, KY: Cengage Learning PTR, 2011.
This book, written by a veteran filmmaker, explores all aspects of digital filmmaking, including sound editing work completed by Foley artists.

ORGANIZATIONS

Association of Motion Picture Sound (AMPS)
27 Old Gloucester Street
London WC1N 3AX
England
+44 (0) 1753 669111
Website: http://www.amps.net/contact
AMPS was founded in 1989 to provide a place where people involved in motion picture and television sound can "exchange information, solve common problems, and keep abreast of rapidly changing technology."

Motion Picture Sound Editors (MPSE)
11712 Moorpark Street, #102
Studio City, CA 91604
Website: http://www.mpse.org
MPSE was founded in 1953 to educate the public and the filmmaking community about the importance of sound editing. Members include sound editors, Foley editors, dialogue editors, and music editors.

PERIODICALS

Independent
PO Box 391620
Cambridge, MA 02139
(877) 513-7400
Website: http://independent-magazine.org
This nonprofit magazine is a source of information for people in the independent, grassroots, and activist media. It shares news information in the film industry, essays, interviews, and reviews.

Mix
28 East 28th Street, 12th floor
New York, NY 10016
(212) 378-0400
Website: http://www.mixonline.com
This high-end audio magazine covers professional recording, music technology, live sound, and film and video production. An online magazine and print magazine are both available.

VIDEOS

"The Foley Artist," *Los Angeles Times*
https://www.youtube.com/watch?v=UNvKhe2npMM
Two Foley artists demonstrate how they make sound
effects for film.

Foley Artists
https://www.youtube.com/watch?v=MHAIgJsMoXw
This video shows how Foley artists re-create sound
effects for film.

APPS

Audio Evolution Mobile
This multitrack audio recorder turns a smart device into a
mobile sound studio. The app can be used to mix, record,
loop playback, and automate and correct sounds.

HiFiCorder
This audio app is ideal for recording and editing.
You can select parts of recordings and make loop
recordings.

WEBSITES

Due to the changing nature of internet links, Rosen Publishing has developed an online list of websites related to the subject of this book. This site is updated regularly. Please use this link to access the list:

http://www.rosenlinks.com/CCWC/enter

GLOSSARY

ACROBAT An entertainer who performs gymnastic feats that require precise control of the body.

AERIALIST A person who performs in the air, high above the ground on tightropes, a trapeze, silks, ropes, and more.

ANIMATION An artistic technique that requires the successive photographing of drawings to show movement.

ANIMATRONICS Robotic puppets that have lifelike movements that are controlled by a human or computer.

BOOM A machine used to reach high objects or lift heavy objects.

CARPENTRY A job or activity that makes or repairs things in wood.

CONTORTIONIST An entertainer who can twist his/her body into unusual positions.

DIALECT A form of language that is specific to a region.

GRIP A member of the stage crew who is responsible for building and maintaining the equipment that holds cameras.

INDEPENDENT CONTRACTOR A person who works independently for a company and is not considered an employee.

MARIONETTES Puppets controlled by a series of strings and wires.

MIME An entertainer who uses actions, gestures, and movements to act a role.

SOUND MIXER Equipment that controls the quality and volume of sound picked up by microphones.

SUPPLEMENTAL Something that is added to something else.

PORTFOLIO A collection of work samples used to get future employment.

POSTPRODUCTION The period of time after a film has been shot with the cameras.

REVENUE The amount of money that a company or person makes.

RIGGER A stage worker who works with ropes, booms, lifts, and hoists.

TRAILER In film, this is an excerpted "commercial" showing highlights from an upcoming movie.

TRAPEZE ARTIST A person who performs on a trapeze, which is a large swinglike apparatus that flies high in the air above a net.

VAUDEVILLE A type of entertainment popular in the early 1900s that included satire, slapstick, song, and dance.

VENTRILOQUIST An entertainer who can speak or make sounds that appear to come from an inanimate object (like a puppet or dummy).

ZUMBA An aerobic form of dancing that includes moves inspired by Latin dance.

BIBLIOGRAPHY

Abbott, Liz. Voiceover Actor, Los Angeles, CA. Personal interview with the author, March 25, 2016.

"Actors." *Occupational Outlook Handbook,* BLS.gov. Last modified December 17, 2015 (http://www.bls.gov/ooh/entertainment-and-sports/actors.htm).

Bloom, Jeff. Los Angeles, CA. Personal interview with the author, March 11, 2016.

Brandon, Kayla. "NFL Cheerleaders Are Raising Their Poms Poms After the Latest News They Got from a Judge." IJReview. com. Retrieved April 5, 2016 (http://www.ijreview.com/2016/01/512082-nfl-cheerleaders-are-rejoicing-after-judge-rules-on-complaints-they-were-underpaid/).

Burke, Monte. "Inside the life of a rodeo clown." *Forbes*, May 5, 2009 (http://www.forbes.com/2009/05/05/rodeo-clown-inside-lifestyle-sports-rodeo-clown.html).

"Dancers and Choreographers." *Occupational Outlook Handbook*, BLS.gov. Last modified December 17, 2015 (http://www.bls.gov/ooh/entertainment-and-sports/dancers-and-choreographers.htm).

"Foley Artistry: The ambient sound effects of Episode 1." Filmsound.org. Retrieved April 4, 2016 (http://filmsound.org/foley/episode1-foley.htm).

Laird, Lisa. Orange City, Iowa. Personal interview with the author, March 20, 2016.

Lovelace, Simon. "Getting into backstage work in the arts." Guardian.com, November 20, 2012 (http://www.theguardian.com/culture-professionals-network/culture-professionals-blog/2012/nov/20/backstage-work-arts-career-tips).

Meservy, April. Provo, UT. Personal interview with the author, April 5, 2016.

MSNBC News. "Cheerleaders speak out over fair pay/Oakland Raiderette, Super Bowl, NFL," YouTube video, 6:21. February 1, 2015 (https://www.youtube.com/watch?v=Jt6dP97IIsU).

"Musicians and Singers." *Occupational Outlook Handbook*, BLS.gov. Last modified December 17, 2015. Retrieved April 4, 2016 (http://www.bls.gov/ooh/entertainment-and-sports/musicians-and-singers.htm#tab-6).

"Our Teachers." Lifehouse Performing Arts Academy. Retrieved April 5, 2016 (http://www.lifehouseacademy.com/our-teachers/).

Prabhakar, Charan, Los Angeles, CA. Personal interview with the author, March 9, 2016.

Reed, Emily, Los Angeles, CA. Personal interview with the author, March 15, 2016.

Siddarth, Vodnala. "Voice-over actors are talking up the apps that help them get work." *Los Angeles Times*, September 8, 2015 (http://www.latimes.com/entertainment/envelope/cotown/la-et-ct-voiceover-tech-20150909-story.html).

Soh, June. "Circus Train is Home to Traveling Performers." *Voice of America*. Last modified May 1, 2012. Retrieved April 5, 2016 (http://www.voanews.com/content/circus-train-is-home-to-traveling-performers-149827935/370274.html).

Time staff. "The 30 Most Influential People on the Internet." *Time*, March 5, 2015 (http://time.com/3732203/the-30-most-influential-people-on-the-internet/).

Toplikar, Dave. "Being a rodeo clown not all funny business." *Las Vegas Sun*, December 6, 2012 (http://lasvegassun.com/news/2012/dec/06/being-rodeo-clown-not-all-funny-business/).

INDEX

ABOUT THE AUTHOR

Amie Jane Leavitt graduated from Brigham Young University and is an accomplished author, researcher, and photographer. She has written more than sixty books for kids, has contributed to online and print media, and has worked as a consultant, writer, and editor for numerous educational publishing and assessment companies. To check out a listing of Amie's current projects and published works, check out her website at www.amiejaneleavitt.com.

PHOTO CREDITS

Designer: Brian Garvey; Editor: Haley E. D. Houseman; Photo Researcher: Bruce Donnola.